The Ultimate Guide to Google AdWords

Unleash the Remarkable Potential to Spell Success

Disclaimer

Summary

Every business owner today is desperately looking for means to survive the aggressive competition and this is where this eBook comes into the picture. This eBook aims to provide an in-depth overview of the advertising mechanism that has taken the world by storm. Yes, we are talking about none other than "Google AdWords".

Starting with the basics, this eBook intends to address tactics that can help any business maximize the effect of its efforts. Discover the power of Google AdWords that you never knew existed and find answers to questions like:

1) What are prospect-winning strategies?
2) How to make your business spectacularly successful with Google AdWords?
3) How to structure a campaign from the scratch?
4) Do keyword tools really work?
5) How to use Google ads to your advantage?
6) How to climb higher on the success ladder with conversion tracking?

In addition, you will uncover secrets for business to cruise along the lines of success. For all this and a lot more, start reading to redefine business success.

Contents

Chapter 01: How to Win Them All - A Strategy to Encourage Prospects to Choose You Over Others

Google is a name that needs no introductions. It has found its way into every single aspect of our lives and the business landscape is no exception. Given its phenomenal influence in the corporate arena, embracing Google for business is inevitable.

Prospects or customers are the life-support system for any business. What makes incorporation of Google into a business's advertising campaign unavoidable is the fact that it can bring you prospects 7 days a week, 365 days a year, round the clock. Such is the power of Google that without it, no business stands a chance to survive in the present day and age.

Getting new prospects is the one obstacle not many learn to overcome. However, with solutions like Google AdWords by your side, you can keep all your worries at bay.

It might be a dream to get targeted customers with minimal investment a few years back but today, thanks to Google AdWords, that dream has found its realization. Hence, it will only be justified to call 'Google AdWords' the most remarkable advertising development of the entire decade.

How to Make Others Find You?

The key to unlocking endless opportunities is not chasing prospects. Instead it's the other way round. Success of a business boils down to the simple idea of 'showing up' when customers are looking for you. If you are showing up at the right time, at the right place for the right people, there is no reason customers won't be interested in whatever it is your business has to offer.

There are millions of users accessing Google search every day. This means that just by using Google AdWords, you can significantly increase your chances of being found when any of the searches, relevant to your business niche, are initiated. Land among the top search engine results and your business will go a long way. All your efforts should be directed at churning out a 'yes' for the following questions.

I.   Are customers finding your website?

II. Are they showing interest in your offerings?

III.   Are they coming back to you?

To accomplish it, leverage the power of Google AdWords. Watch the profits pouring in and brace yourself for the flood of customers that Google AdWords is going to send your way.

Chapter 02: Transform Your Business into a Money Making Machine

Now that you have realized the significance of landing among the first few pages of search results, the next step is selling your offering on the internet. It is no rocket-science. Just incorporate all the important elements and nothing can stop your website from being a simple, profitable and thriving one.

Get the Wheels Going When Customers Start Searching

When a customer initiates a search, the potential of the business is to nail him then and there. This can easily be understood with the following example.

Sam initiates a search for 'facial wrinkles' and this is what Google displayed in response to the search query.

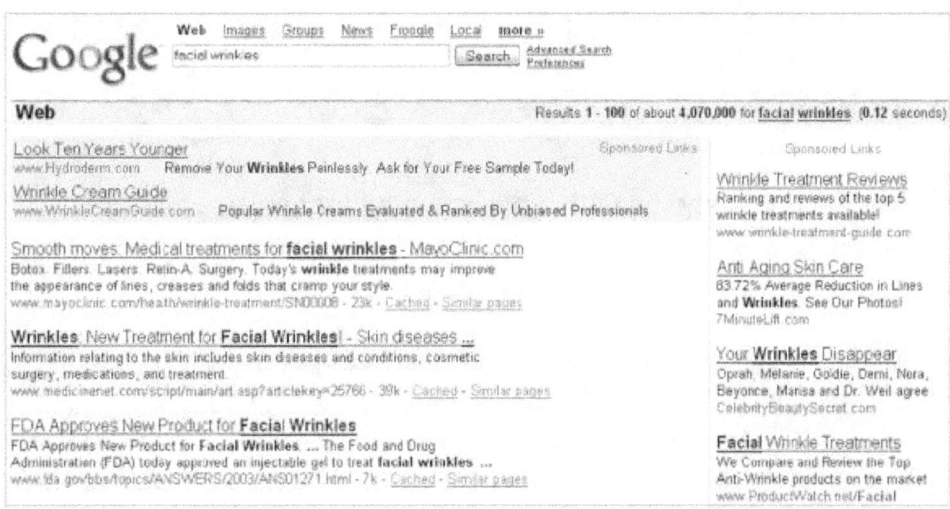

On the right and top of the page, AdWords ads are displayed. These are paid ads and the left side of the page demonstrates search listings that are for free. Now, Sam clicks on the first option that says:

Wrinkle Treatment Reviews

Ranking and Review of the Top 5 Wrinkle Treatments Available!

Wrinkle-Treatment-Guide.Com

Or Sam is surfing the web. She lands at www.PriceGrabber.com and is reading review of a recently published guide on cosmetic surgery.

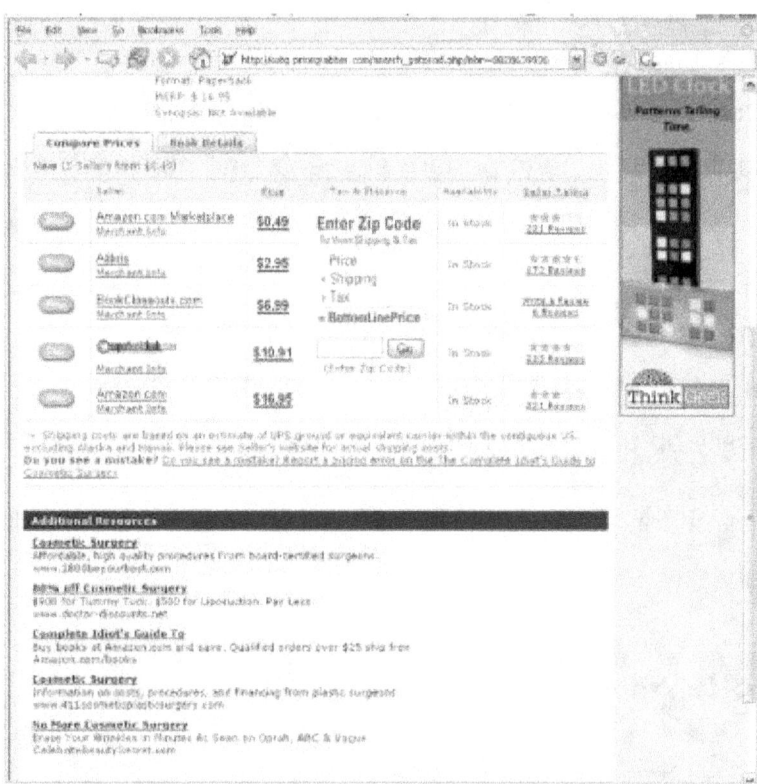

At the bottom of the page, she finds this attractive ad that says:

Cosmetic Surgery

Affordable, High Quality Procedures from Board-Certified Surgeons

Www.100beautyproducts.Com

This ad is displayed by the Google Adsense program and must be listed on hundreds or thousands of websites. The ad interests her. She clicks on the advertisement and is routed to the following page.

From this point there are only three things that can happen:

a) Sam makes a decision to purchase
b) Sam asks for more information
c) Sam leaves

It is a more feasible approach for certain websites to offer information instead of a product. This can be done by simply asking Sam for her email address and in return for her little effort, she will be getting a report, guide, white paper or anything that can help address her needs. This can be an absolutely rewarding strategy provided your customer's problems, such as 'wrinkles' will continue for a while and will not end with a single buy.

By collecting email addresses of several other Sams, you can effortlessly create a priceless email list. So, the next time Sam lands on your website, she may leave for the time being but she will come back later after asking for more information. If she comes to you twice, she will come to you in future as well and you can pat your back as you have not only addressed your customer's need and moved stuff from your shelf to hers but has also earned a customer for life.

Your Mission- Where to Focus Your Google AdWords Campaign

A lot of advertising campaigns do not deliver desired results. This failure can be attributed to the lack of understanding of the concept that if you are buying clicks at a rate of $1, you should be making $2 at least while Sam or any other customer is on your website. You can only achieve that cut above your competitors by making more money from clicks than they are.

Tools You Can't Afford To Miss

Regardless of what you are selling, there are certain tools that are principal to every business existence.

a) Domain name

b) Business website

c) Email with an auto responder service

d) Service of shopping cart

e) Products

f) A Google AdWords account

Setup a website, open a Google AdWords account and start racking profits higher than ever before. Are you already excited about the idea? Keep reading to outpace your competition and get your business the limelight it deserves.

Google has completely revamped Google Adwords, and is in the process of updating all of its products as well, giving them a completely new look. The basic aim of Google is to create a consistent look across all the servers and web, while ensuring that the entire interface is user friendly, thereby enabling the users to have a pleasant experience. The new Adword makes use of more screen, and allows more room for tools and reports to appear on the screen, thereby allowing the user to plan and implement campaigns accordingly.

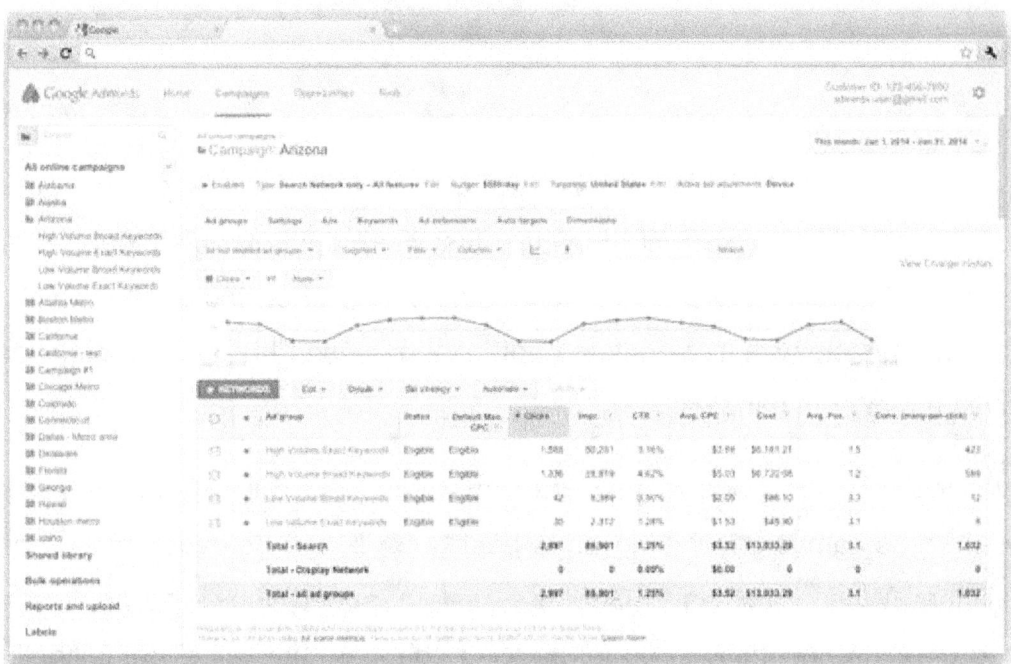

Chapter 03: Breathing Life into Your Google Campaign

Nothing can be more annoying than making a website and keeping your fingers crossed, hoping that customers will show up. Just when marketers felt that there was no ray of hope left for them, pay-per-click marketing emerged on the scene. This modern-day marketing miracle with its unraveled potential promised businesses highly targeted traffic within a matter of minutes.

After investing a few minutes of your precious time, you will not be witnessing your Google AdWords campaign working at its best but will also be receiving a reasonable flow of visitors. When it comes to Google's system, speed knows no bounds and it is this speed of doing new things and introducing changes that will eventually allow your efforts to pay off.

From 'No Prospects' To 'Know Your Prospects'

Since prospects are the lifeline for any success, it is crucial to know your target market and to determine where it resides. As far as pay-per-click is concerned, it is not an exception watching money go down the drain. You picked up a keyword, created an ad but no one wants to buy from you. Keep the following questions in mind to avoid attracting wrong kind of traffic for your business.

How Many People Are Looking For This Product?

Here you have to estimate your traffic realistically. The previous chapter showed the example of Dremu Skincare. Now let's assume, the owner wants more traffic for his website through Google, what should he do?

First and foremost, he should start off by making a list of possible keywords all relevant to his business offerings. This may include words like dermatology, anti-aging or wrinkles. Now, using any keyword selector tool, it is possible to find out how many searches have been initiated for a particular keyword. Keywords with highest search ratio can be the key players. In addition, since different users use alternative terms for the same product, they have to be determined as well.

With the right keywords, it is possible for a website to inspire thousands of searches. However, these searches come at a price.

In Market Targeting

This is another feature that is related to the display ads feature. This feature is listed under the tab of "Interest Categories", this targeting tool allows you to target those visitors of your website who look like they are seriously considering purchasing your product or service. This tool helps you to analyze the habit of the customer and based on the behavioral pattern, the visitor to the website is exhibiting; it calculates whether the visitor is considering your product or service offering, is serious about making a purchase, or if the visitor is simply passing through.

This helps you in creating strategies for targeting those visitors who have your product in their consideration set and are thinking of buying it. This tool is extremely beneficial for all marketers, which can then get the data of those people who have the potential to become their loyal customers.

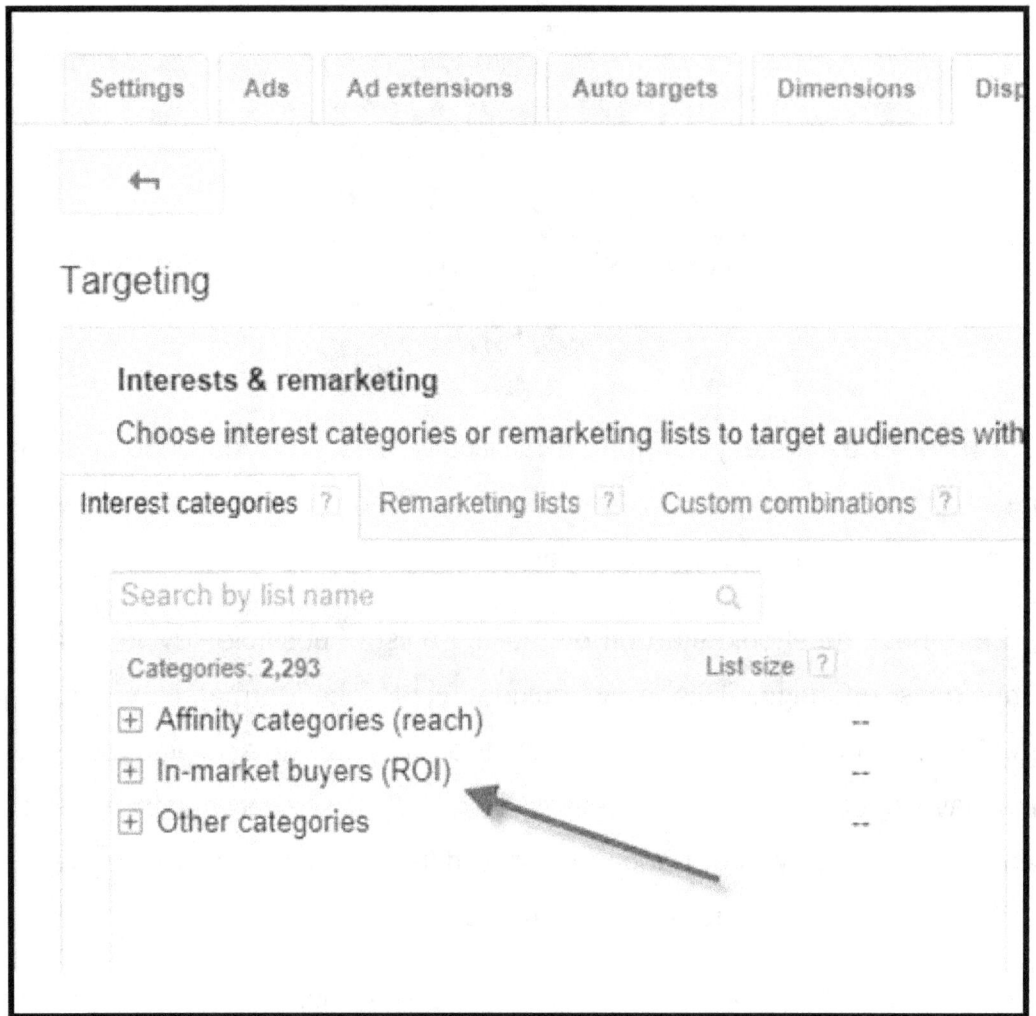

What Is The Cost Of Your Clicks?

If you wish to determine the cost of your click, it depends on the ad position. The top position is known to generate most clicks. Google can inform you about it. Just select on the option 'Want to Purchase Most Clicks Possible'.

> **What is the maximum you are willing to pay each time someone clicks on your ad?**
>
> You influence your ad's position by setting its maximum cost per click (CPC) [?]. The max CPC is the highest willing to pay each time a user clicks on your ad. Your max CPC can be changed as often as you like
>
> Enter your maximum CPC: $ [_____] (Minimum $0.01)
> Higher CPCs lead to higher ad positions, which usually get more clicks.
>
> Want to purchase the most clicks possible?
>
> ▶ View Traffic Estimator - Enter a CPC and see the estimated rank, traffic, and costs for your keyword(s).
>
> **Three things to remember:**
>
> - Your ads won't start running until you activate your account by responding to an email we'll send you. Y always change your CPC and budget, or pause your account entirely.
> - Your budget controls your spending. If your daily budget is $5.00 and there are 30 days in a month, you charged more than $150 in that month.
> - If the estimates on this page seem high, you may have chosen keywords that are too broad or competit your costs by choosing more specific keywords, like *red roses* instead of *flowers*. Specific keywords ar likely to turn a click into a customer. Edit your keyword list.

Just below this screen, you will find Google Traffic Estimator telling you about the traffic, cost and rank for your keywords.

a. How to Know Your Competitors?

As far as Google is concerned, ads are displayed at the right hand side and upper left side of the page. In order to find out how many advertisers are competing against your chosen keyword, keep in mind the topmost ad. Now go through all the search pages that exist and continue until the same ad is displayed again. The number of ads you come across before the one on top is repeated is the number of advertisers competing against you for a particular keyword.

Google usually displays around 11 ads per page. It will, therefore, only work in your favor to target the top eight positions or to pay a cost per click high enough to stay there.

Setting Up Your Campaign

To start your advertising campaign with Google AdWords, go to the link https://AdWords.google.com. You will land at the following page.

For free setup support
call **1-800-919-9922** or request a callback   **START NOW**

AdWords

Advertise your business on Google

No matter what your budget, you can display your ads on Google and our advertising network.
Pay only if people click your ads.

Sign in   Google

Email

Password

Sign in   ✓ Stay signed in

Can't access your account?

AdWords helps customers find us for their spring gardening needs.

General Manager, Evergreen Nursery

How it works	You create your ads
	You create ads and choose keywords, which are words or phrases related to your business. Get keyword ideas
Reach more customers	
Costs and payment	**Your ads appear on Google**
	When people search on Google using one of your keywords, your ad may appear next to the search results. Now you're advertising to an audience that's already interested in you.
For local businesses	
Success stories	**You attract customers**
	People can simply click your ad to make a purchase or learn more about you.

Keywords are what people search for on Google.

Sign up now

Your ad appears beside relevant search results.

TD-100110820.jpg   TD-10047447.jpg   TD-100113190.jpg

Now try to locate the button 'Click to begin'. Select it.

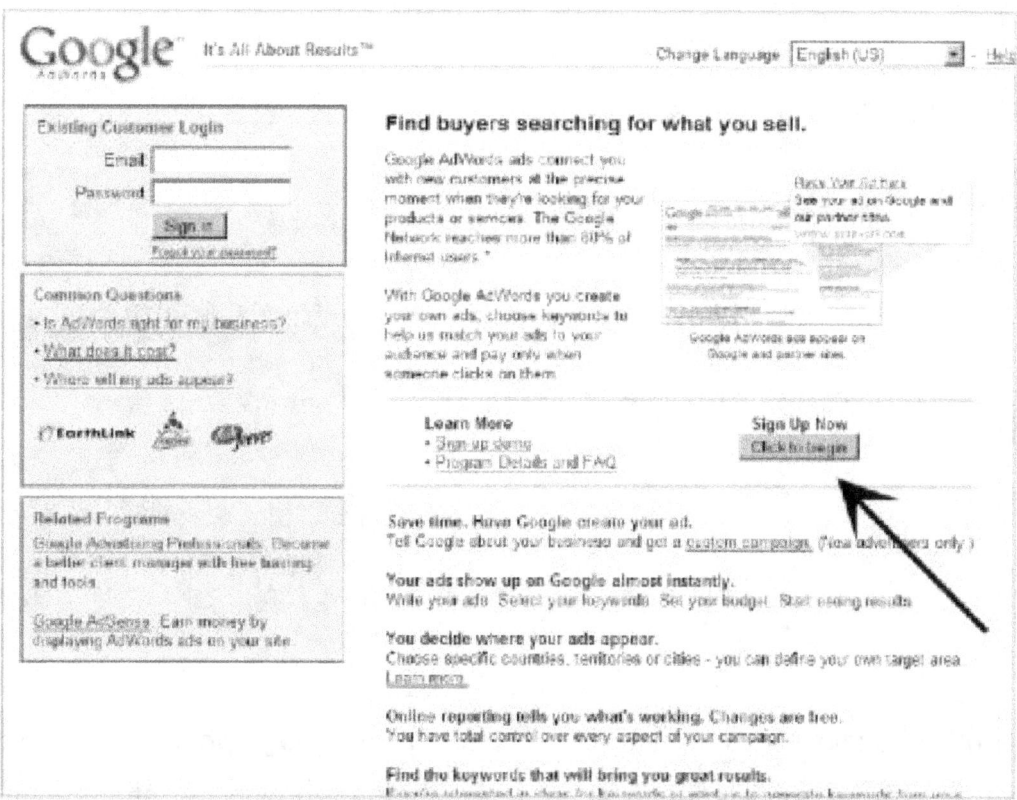

We will now provide you with the insight to setup you account using the 'standard edition'.

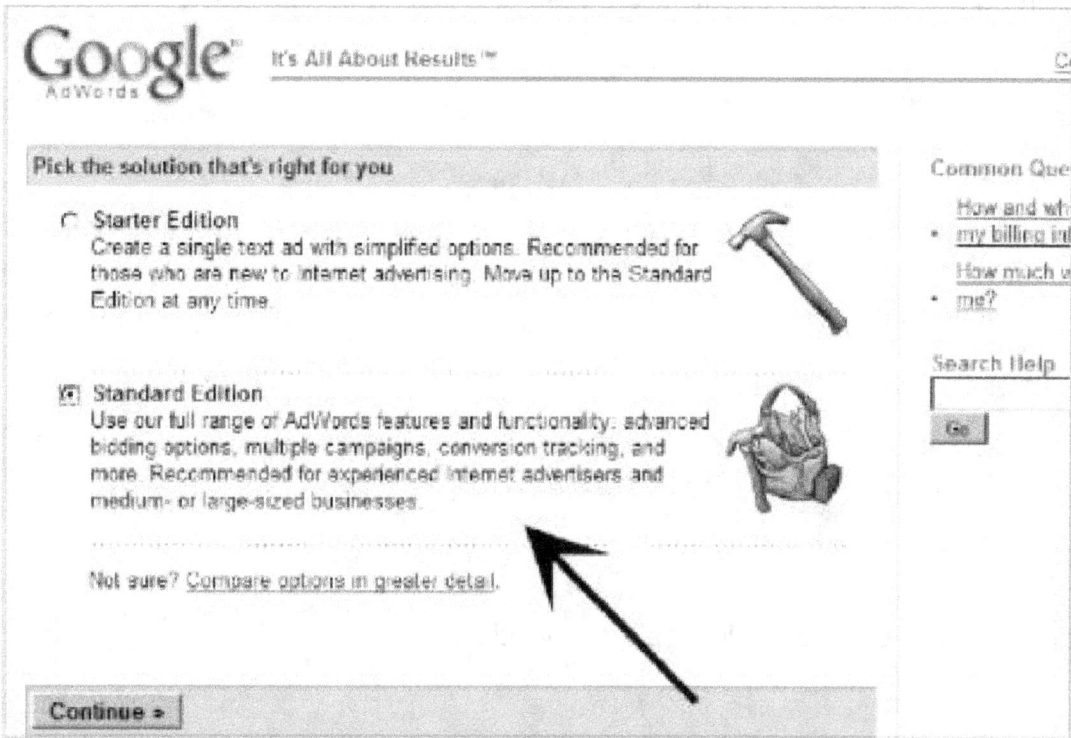

Select Location and Language

Select the languages you want to target.

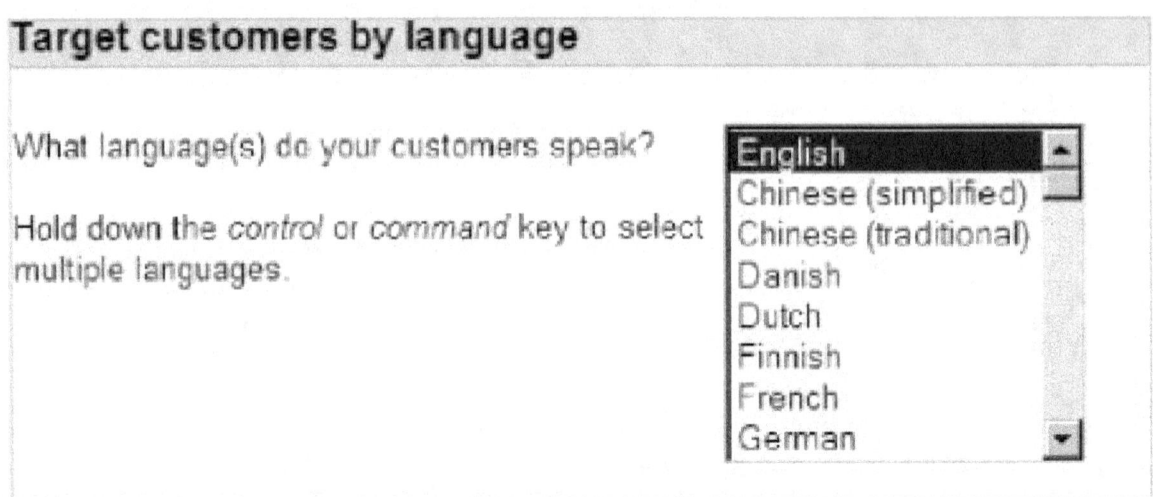

Google AdWords allow the targeting of prospects using geographic areas as well. You can decide to target entire countries, particular regions, provinces, states or cities. In addition, you can also select geographic areas that are custom-designated by providing information such as coordinates of longitude-latitude. You can even custom-target by specifying a radius around certain kilometers or miles of an address.

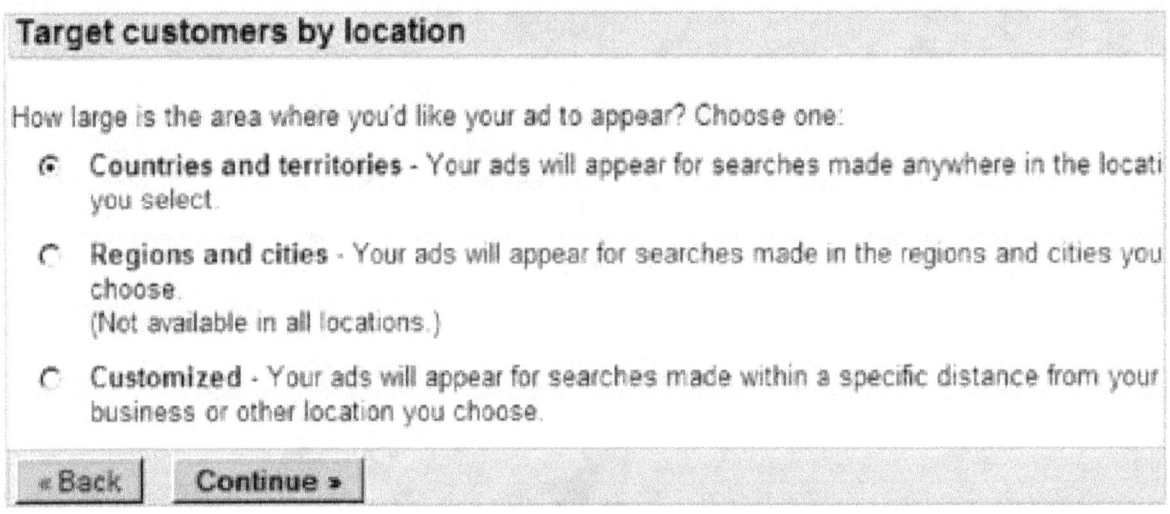

Select one or more countries to display your ads.

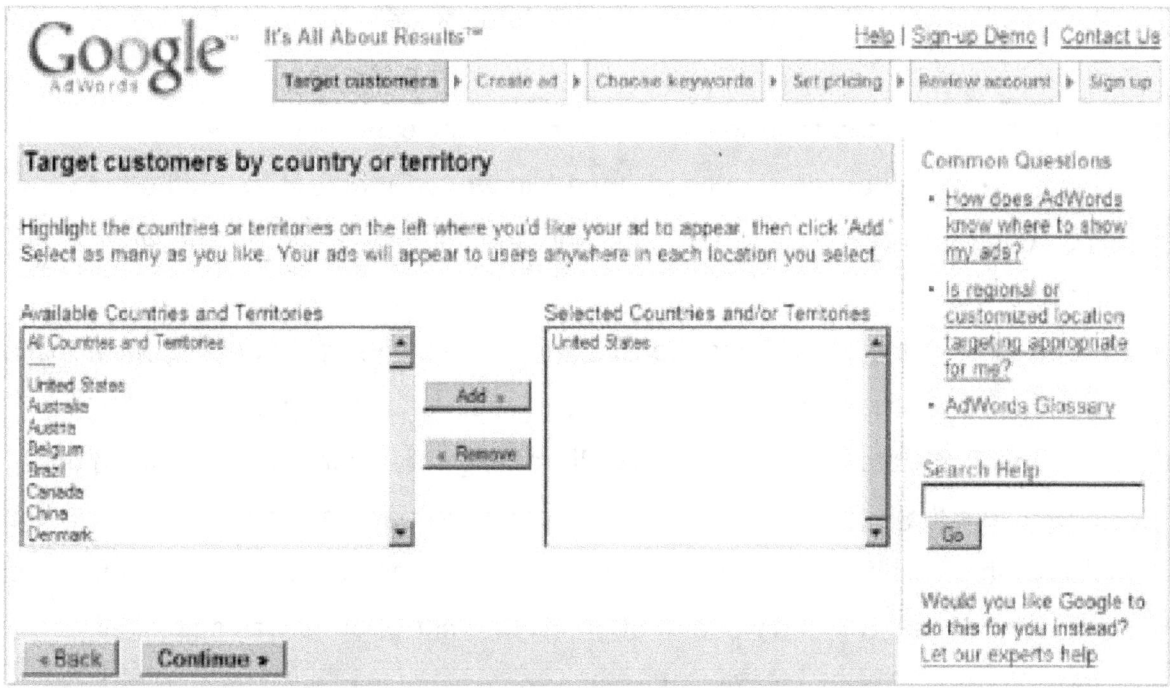

Writing Your First Ad

This page will be displayed to you for writing your first ad.

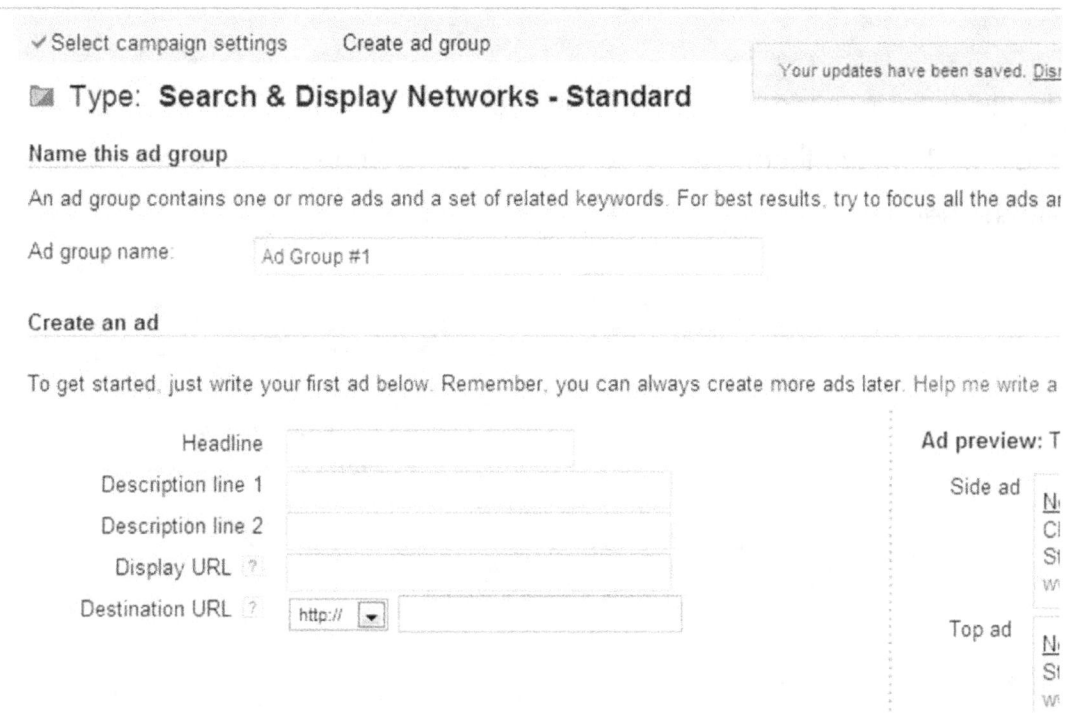

When writing an ad, some points to keep in mind are as follows.

I. Include keyword(s) in the headline as customers are most likely to click on such ads.

II. List a benefit on the second line for your ad to succeed.

III. Increase your chances of success by adding an offer or feature on the third line. You can test reverse the order of second and third line to determine what works best for you.

IV. Fourth line of the ad includes the URL. It can be a specific page on your website but does not necessarily have to be a particular landing page.

V. The last line states the destination URL routing customers to your landing page.

VI. Make sure the last line directs user to a particular page and not your home page. A customer will be more than frustrated to find out he has made all the effort just to land on a page with a world of offerings and not what he was specifically looking for.

In addition, if you intend to generate more clicks, test more ads against the one you just created.

Inserting Keywords

Now is the time to insert keywords. It is recommended to start with two only. Don't forget to put [ ] around them so as to only get traffic that has typed in the exact words in the search query.

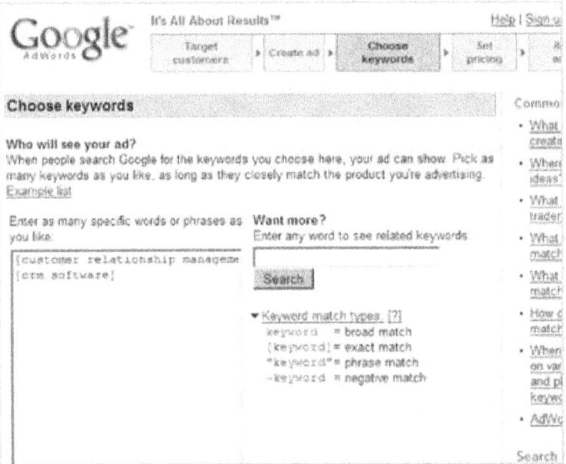

Initially it is not a good practice to use hundreds and thousands of words to generate traffic. Start off with the most important ones and build your success from there.

Sitelinks Enhanced

A brilliant new feature that allows advertisers greater control over the appearance of their advertisements, it is a great addition to Google Adwords. You can customize your advertisements to portray different messages during different times of the day. You can also design the sitelinks differently for different devices, even catered to various mobile devices. This provides advertisers and marketers with an opportunity to provide user related context in their advertisements. Now you also have the option of analyzing the performance of individual sitelinks, whereas, previously it could only be done on groups.

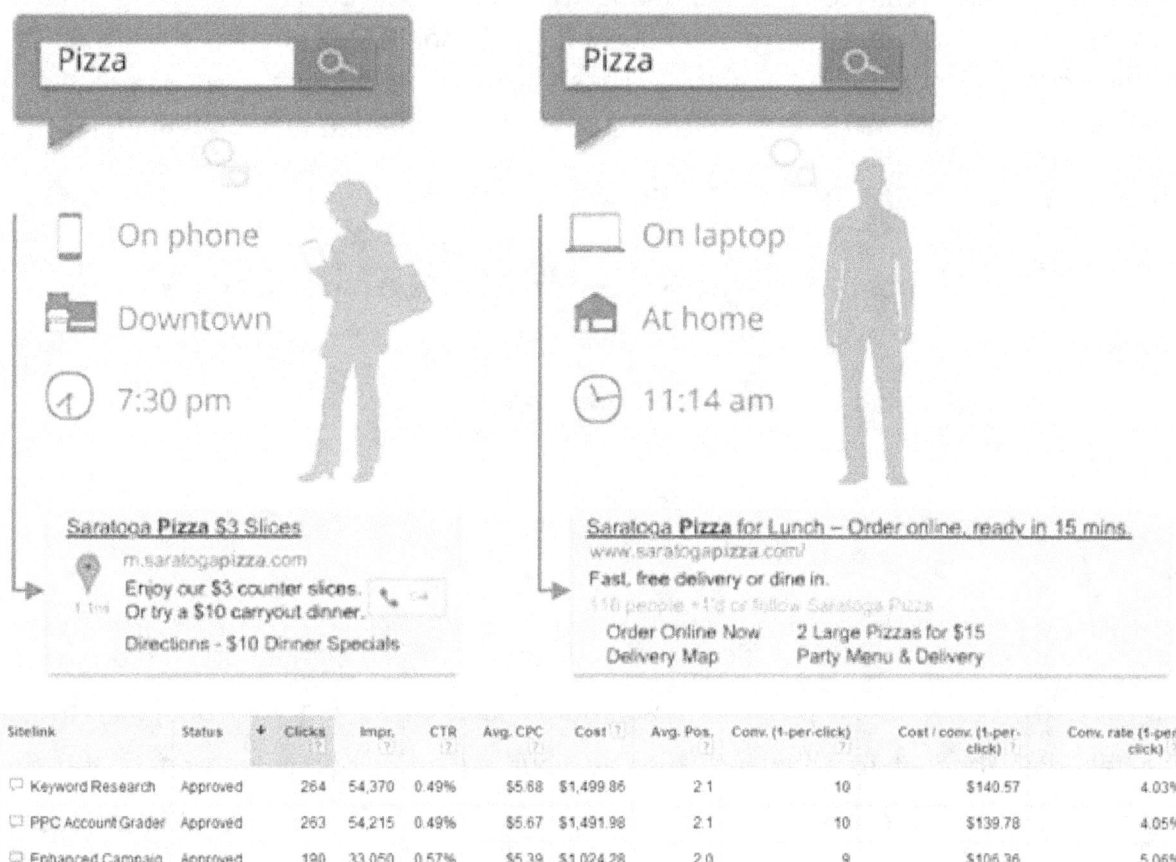

Sitelink	Status	Clicks	Impr.	CTR	Avg. CPC	Cost	Avg. Pos.	Conv. (1-per-click)	Cost / conv. (1-per-click)	Conv. rate (1-per-click)
Keyword Research	Approved	264	54,370	0.49%	$5.68	$1,499.86	2.1	10	$140.57	4.03%
PPC Account Grader	Approved	263	54,215	0.49%	$5.67	$1,491.98	2.1	10	$139.78	4.05%
Enhanced Campaigns?	Approved	190	33,050	0.57%	$5.39	$1,024.28	2.0	9	$106.36	5.06%
Latest Case Study	Approved	119	24,344	0.49%	$5.67	$674.40	2.1	5	$128.86	4.39%
Total - all sitelinks		264	54,377	0.49%	$5.68	$1,499.86	2.1	10	$140.57	4.03%

Enhanced Campaigns

This feature makes mobile advertisement easier and simpler to implement. The updated design the first change, which appeals to and attracts the mind of every marketer. The impact of this change has been seen to have affected everyone who has and Adwords account.

The advertisements have become smarter as Google allows them to be matched to the device, which is used to perform the search for a product or service. This gives the ads a user context, which is much needed by all marketing efforts. The marketer gets numerous chances for better ad messaging as the location of the searcher, the device used to search and the time, at which it was all searched can lead to a compelling consumer insight for all marketers and business people. Through one campaign such compelling insights can be obtained, along with impressive consumer buying behavior data that the advertisers can create desktop and mobile advertisements, which are catered to targeting a specific audience. These advertisements can also be presented in intelligent and unique ways while delivering relevant information to the consumer.

Choosing Currency and Setting up Daily Budget

What is the most you would like to spend, on average, per day?

The daily budget [?] controls your costs. When the daily limit is reached, on average, your ad will stop showing for that day. (The budget controls the frequency of your ad, not its position.) Raise or lower your budget as often as you like.

Enter your daily budget: $ |

You have to keep things wallet-friendly. If you can afford $70 instead of $150 dollars per day, cut down on your bid prices or else you will end up cutting your budget. You can use the daily budget tool that will display your ad for a particular part of the day. Positions that are lower lead to more conversions and it is more rational to be seen at bottom on a page than being at the top after having to trim your budget.

Product Listing Advertisements

Product listing advertisements have gone local, which allows the searchers to locate your product and services close to their home. Depending on what a consumer searches for, the product listings allow them to find out whether the product or service they have searched for is available in nearby, local stores. All the searcher has to do is click on the advertisement; the user is taken to a page, which contains all of the essential information about the product or service, from availability to the stock, which is present in the store. This program is available to a select few merchants, who should at least have 10 stores to become eligible for it.

Shopping Campaigns

On February 18 2014, Google announced that shopping campaigns are officially available to all of the advertisers, no matter in which part of the world they be. This new shopping campaign provides a different way of targeting products, which is more retail in nature. It also allows for more robust reporting, along with providing competitive insights, which were previously not available.

This effort will help in solving many problems with retailers, particularly for those who want to target at a more granular level. The added features will helps the users of Google Adwords manage their products by excluding and prioritizing them, as they want. Along with this, it will also help the users see the increase in their return on investment on their PLAs in the future.

Setting Maximum Cost per Click

Set the high limit for your budget now. Since each keyword caters to a different market, each one of them will have a bid price. Google allows you to set bids for each individual keyword later.

What is the maximum you are willing to pay each time someone clicks on your ad?

You influence your ad's position by setting its maximum cost per click (CPC) [?]. The max CPC is the highest price you're willing to pay each time a user clicks on your ad. Your max CPC can be changed as often as you like.

Enter your maximum CPC. $ [   ] (Minimum: $0.01)
Higher CPCs lead to higher ad positions, which usually get more clicks.

If you opt for the 'Want to Purchase The Most Possible Clicks?' link, Google will display the highest bid for a particular keyword. While this is terribly expensive and may drive irrelevant traffic, it will ensure that your ad is displayed at the most prominent position.

Review Everything

Once all is done, check your keywords, ads, daily-budget, cost-per-click and watch your campaign climb its way to success.

Entering Email Address

You will receive an email from Google including a special link. By clicking on the link, Google ensures that the login information you provided is valid.

Enter Your Billing Information

As soon as your payment information is confirmed, you ads will start displaying. You are now all set to give your competitors a run for their money.

By following the steps listed above, you will soon be creating a custom-tailored campaign for your targeted demographics. It will reflect your business personality with your fingerprint all over it and it will only be a matter of time before success will be yours to claim.

Chapter 04: Tailoring Your Campaign - How to Make the Most Out Of It

'Maximum clicks with minimal investment' is a dream for every business owner. This is often not accomplished for the following reasons.

1. Improperly organized campaigns
2. Lacks of understanding about ad groups

This chapter will educate you on these two crucial aspects.

Change in the Ad Rank

The extensions of ads are an extremely important part of successful advertising campaigns. Not only do they allow you to interact with your potential customer, but also to engage them, the moment your link appears as one of the results on the Google page. They also play a significant part in how high your ads are ranked. In January Google Adwords featured two log posts, in which it described how site links work, and everything else there is to know about site links. It also explained that from then on ads will start playing a significant role in how well the ads are performed, which will ultimately affect their ranking.

In this extension Google encourages all, who use Adwords, to make optimal use of extensions. The reason behind this is that ad extensions help in improving click through rates, along with the overall performance of the ad, thereby, making the ads more useful. The benefits users stand to gain by making full use of extensions are many, which is why Google encourages every one of its users to make complete use of these extensions. Results indicate that many of the users, who have used different extensions, have seen improvements of 10%-20%.

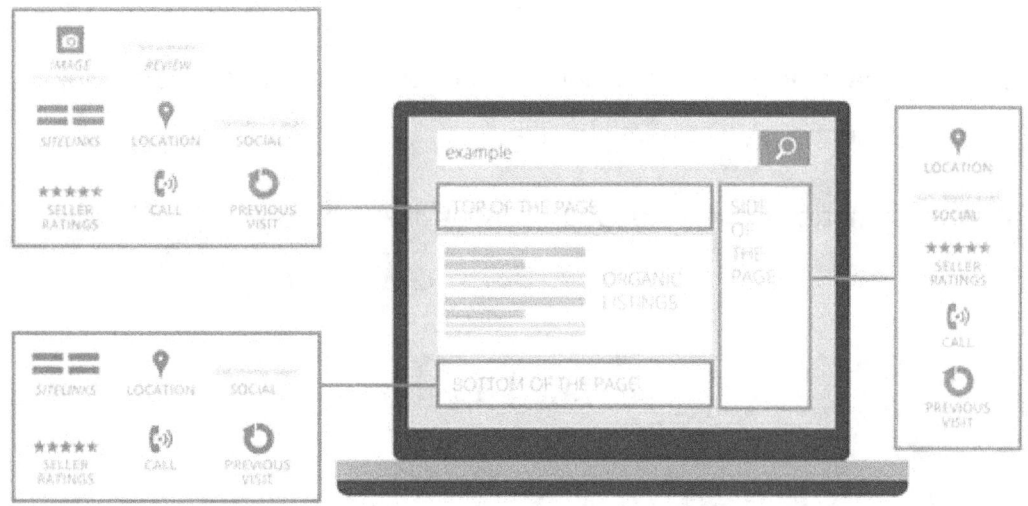

Google Ad Groups Don'ts- Actions to Avoid

Initially most campaigns look a lot like this

Smart Attire

Best choice for all your clothing needs

www.SmartAttire.com

Hats

Tank Tops

Tees

Hoodies

Cardigan

Denim

Shoes

Accessories

The URL will be sending users to a home page will all sorts of diverse links such as 'Home', 'Blog', 'Collections', 'Contact Us', etc.

Their AdWords campaign, when mapped, will look like this:

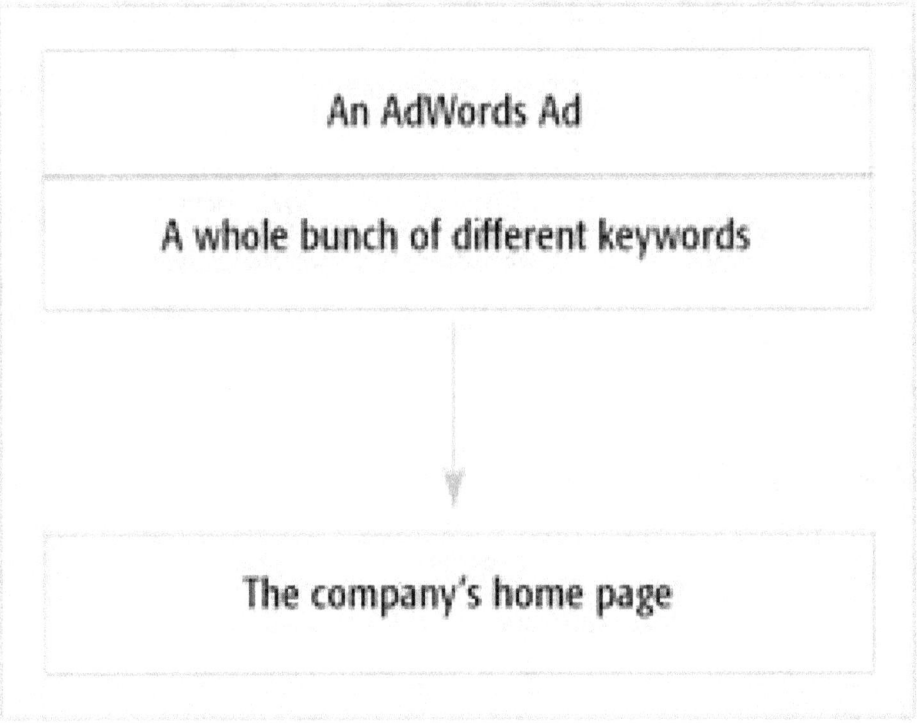

This campaign is doomed for the following reasons.

a) Too many different keywords have been added in the same group.

b) The keywords don't match the ad.

c) A headline with nothing besides the business name is a lousy idea. The CTR will be low and bid price will be higher.

d) This ad is more about 'Smart Attire' and not about customer needs. In short, it won't sell.

e) Landing people on the home page is equivalent to losing a customer for good. If customers have to further search for their needs even after coming to your website, you make them put a lot of effort which is something customers won't appreciate.

On the other hand, a well- crafted campaign will look as follows.

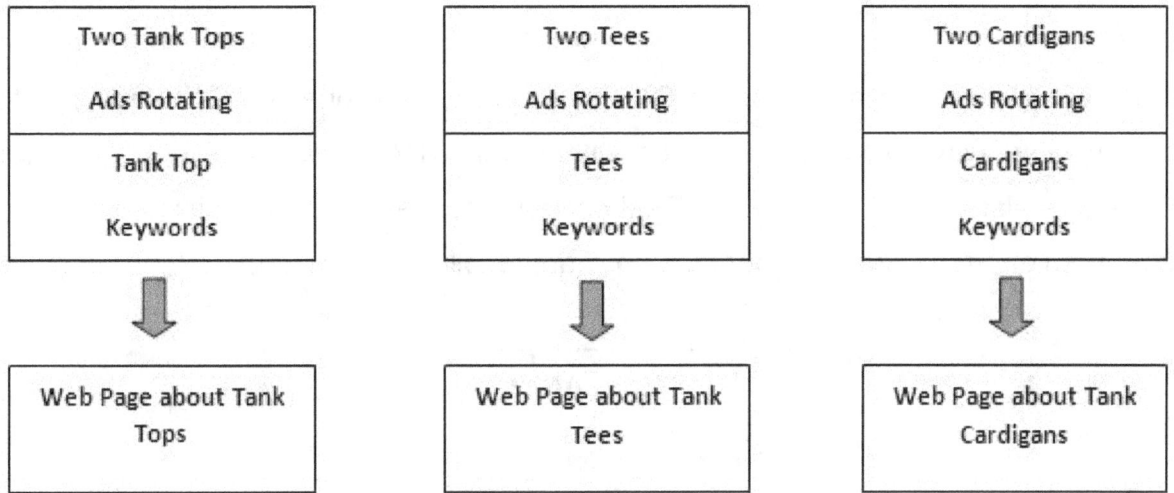

Now your job is to determine the highly targeted terms for each of your keywords and use them to your advantage. There are certain online tools that can help you determine a list of keywords that can work wonders for you.

Don't Ignore Negative Keywords

Before you move ahead with your campaign, find out negative words for your business. It is obvious that there will be a certain market that you do not want to target. For instance, you won't want someone to come to you looking for discounts on clothing, designer's belts or watches, or even sport shoes when all you are offering are stilettos. Hence your list of negative words can be as follows.

a) Discount

b) Designer watches

c) Designer belts 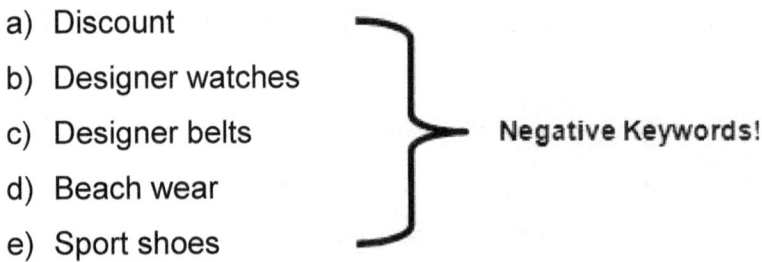 **Negative Keywords!**

d) Beach wear

e) Sport shoes

When you will organize your ad campaign, each one of the negative keywords will go into a variety of groups with a set of its own ads.

Testing Your Ads

To drive better results and improve CTR, write more than one ad. Google will rotate them continuously. Discard the ones with lower CTR. Keep on experimenting to witness consistent improvement in CTR. Long term success with advertising campaigns come from efforts to beat your best ad. Look at the following example.

> **Smart Attire**
> Pep Up Your Look
> Get Cardigans At Unbelievable Prices!
> www.SmartAttire.com/Cardigans

> **Smart Attire**
> Turn heads and inspire envy
> With High quality Cardigans
> www.SmartAttire.com/Cardigans

Both these ads will have a different CTR. Always run two ads for the same category of offerings or products and all your efforts should be focused at surpassing the CTR for your best running ad. Remember, you are your own competition!

In addition, it can be clearly seen that the ads have been written in complete accordance with the ad-writing guidelines defined in the previous chapter. This is what we have done with the ads above.

a) A list of keywords is generated: cardigans, tank tops, tees.

b) Research tools are used to determine variations for these keywords.

c) Every keyword goes into its own family.

d) Two ads are rotated at the same time while making attempts to beat the best.

When visitors click on the link, they are taken to a specific page offering them exactly what they asked for in a query and not to the home page. Another example to understand keyword and campaign grouping better is as follows. This is for terms related to martial arts.

Organize Your Campaigns and Ad Groups

	Campaign #1 Self Defense	Campaign #2 Martial Arts	Campaign #3 Fighting	Campaign #4 Security & Safety	Campaign #5 Protection
Ad Group #1	Women's Self Defense	Karate	Wrestling	Personal Safety	Self Protection
Ad Group #2	Defense Class	Tae Kwon Do	Grappling	Women's Safety	Women's Protection
Ad Group #3	Defense Video	Aikido	Hand-to-Hand Combat	Personal Security	Child Protection
Ad Group #4	Defense Tactic	Hapkido	Weapons Combat	Children's Security	Assault protection

Organize your campaign as suggested above and you will never again have to worry about getting enough clicks or sufficient traffic.

Unveil the Secret to Higher CTR

Just get rid of irrelevant keywords and your CTR will instantly spike. Often during the process of keyword collection, we bid on terms that simply do not belong with our business. They can easily be identified as they often generate zero clicks, gravely damaging the average CTR.

☐ [religion during the renaissance]		0
☐ [ancient greece religion]		0
☐ "hindu religion"		0
☐ "ancient egypt religion"		0
☐ "losing my religion lyrics"		0
☐ [asian religions]		0
☐ [mesopotamia religion]		0

Moving Keywords for a Higher CTR

Improvements in the CTR can be secured with minimal effort. All you have to do is to find keywords generating the highest CTR, pull them out of their group and place them into a new ad group followed by a highly targeted ad. You will be impressed with how good you are at it and it won't take more than a few minutes. It can be better demonstrated with the following examples.

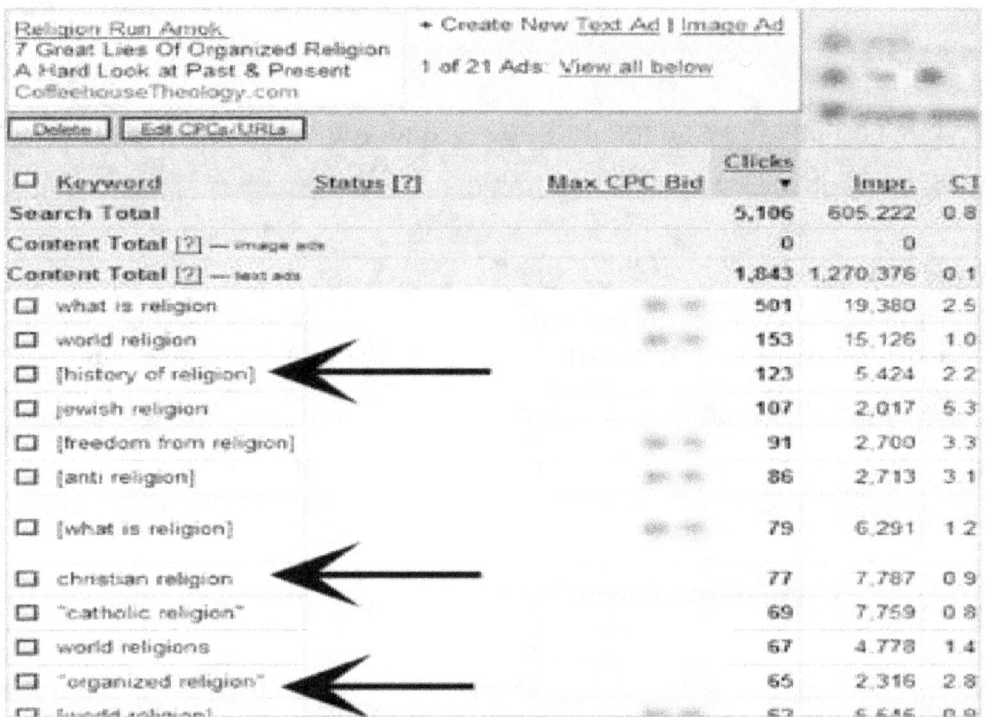

The phenomenal improvements secured in the CTR for the keywords are highlighted below.

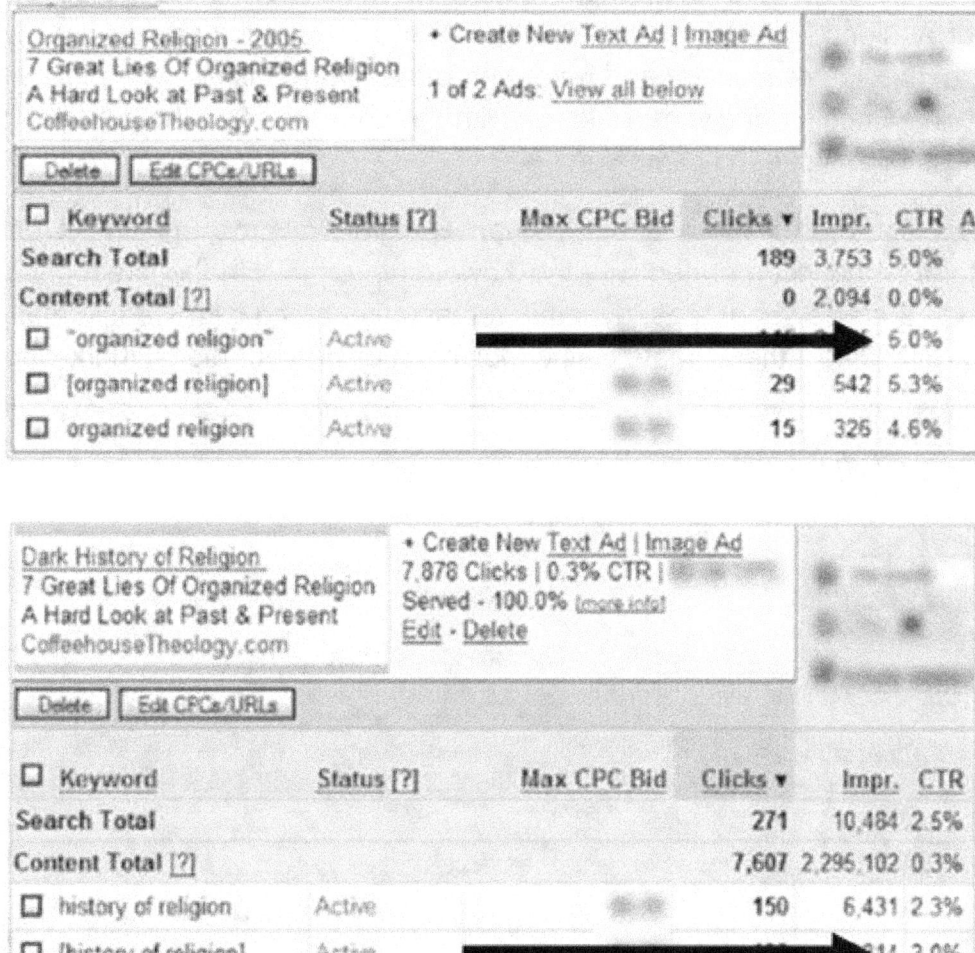

Get more profits in your pockets with the strategies listed above.

Google Analytics – Improved Dynamic Remarketing

Since the beginning of 2012, remarketing is being done with the help of Google analytics. However, only a few people realize the potential this tool holds for creating new target audiences, tapping untapped markets and creating campaigns, which are directed at the target audience. There are more than 250 dimensions, which are available in Google analytics, along with metrics, which help determine the effectiveness of a marketing campaign.

This tool is considered more effective than Google Adwords, making it one of the reasons for it being incorporated with the Adwords efforts. With the latest development, only through a single set of tags, dynamic remarketing along with Google analytics can be powered, making it the ultimate online tool for studying your digital marketing efforts.

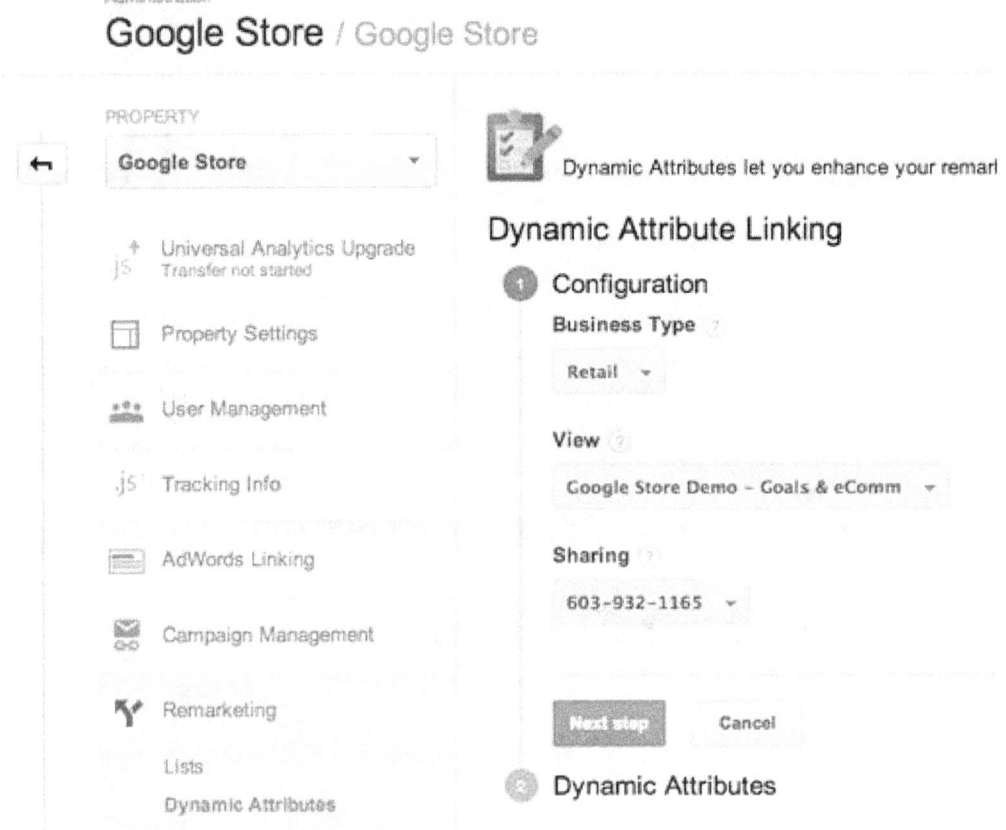

Chapter 05: The ABC of Google Ads That Work

Success of any advertising campaign depends on writing an ad that makes people click. Ads are a chance for businesses to communicate to their prospects. For this reason, they should be compelling enough to inspire the kind of excitement that makes a customer find out more.

Let's assume you have done sufficient keyword research, have a reasonably profitable product to sell and a decent page. At this point, all you need is to put meat around the idea of making Google ads that work.

Become Your Customer

Ads fail to deliver the desired results because we view things from a business perspective. Instead, you have to get into customer's shoes to have him eating out of your hand. Be critical of your own offerings. Find out would you be willing to invest into a product had you been the customer?

The seller should understand that when it comes to making a purchase, a customer has two strong triggers or motivators: avoiding pain or gaining pleasure. Find out how your product can help customers avoid something painful or unpleasant or list how it can help them gain pleasure.

The most crucial obstacle a business has to overcome is to know its target audience's mindset because once that is accomplished, one will be able to create an ad that sells itself inspiring easy money and more clicks.

ABC of Ads

We call it the 'ABC' of ads as these three alphabets perfectly describe the purpose each line should serve. Let's explore them in detail.

a) A For Attention

The first line, or the headline, should simply be a real attention grabber. It should have the potential to subtly encourage the customer to read the rest.

b) B For Benefit

What is the benefit that a customer will get out of your product? Give your prospects a strong reason to buy from you. This would most likely be something that helps one avoid pain or gain pleasure.

c) C For Call to Action

Once a customer reads your ad, the story does not end there. You have to compel your prospects to click.

These three elements can make or break any ad and when done incorrectly, can bring a flourishing ad campaign down on its knees.

A Is For Attention...

It is no secret that the headline is the most crucial aspect of your ad. You have to nail customers then and there or else you don't stand any chances for survival. Some tips to make killer headlines to lend your ads that irresistible appeal are as follows.

a) Capitalize fancy words particularly the first letter.

b) Use numbers whenever possible. Inserting number into your headlines will catch eye instantly because numbers are more likely to stand out from all the text the eye sees.

c) Don't forget to use keywords in headlines. Google displays keywords in bold print if a certain keyword matches a term in search query.

d) Create curiosity, interest, desire, hope, just make your readers feel something when they read your ad headline.

Use the 25 characters in the headline the best way you can as it is your chance to stand out from the crowd. People usually scan the text they see online. You headline should be compelling to the point that the reader stop scanning and start reading instantly.

B Is For Benefit...

The first line of description is where you should convince a potential prospect why he should consider your offering/product by telling him what benefits are in it for him? While first golden rule was 'become your customer'. The second is 'what's the benefit for me?'

This is the most important angle as at the end of the day, it is all a prospect cares about. If your product has some significant benefit to offer, no matter what, customers will buy it.

Emotions drive decisions, period. Give audience a clear idea of what your product has in store for them. By incorporating these rules in your ad, you not only improve chances of getting clicks drastically but your ad will also ignite the kind of interest that encourages prospects to buy.

C Is For Call To Action...

Call to action is usually the third line of the ad. While it is not the same as a call to action one comes across in a sales letter, its importance cannot be denied. Google has certain policies that define what one can and cannot say in a call to action line. It is, therefore, advised to familiarize oneself with these guidelines.

Call to action is important because when all is said and done, the customer should not be wondering 'what's next?' There are certain ads where you cannot include a call to action and for all such ads, the third line should state additional benefits. For the rest, a call to action can serve as that icing on the cake.

Others - Things to Tweak

Things you must consider before writing an ad for Google.

i.   Only one exclamation mark is allowed. Make sure you use it where it matters most.

ii. Incorrect spellings or bad grammar are not tolerated by Google. In the event of any such errors, your ad will simply be rejected.

Real Life Examples

Let's take a look at some examples from real life.

Another example:

The first ad is a great one as it complies with the ABCs defined above. The only problem with the first ad is the 'check out my story' line. Does it ring a bell for the customer? Probably not! Remember the customer does not care about you. It should be about him. As far as the second ad goes, the continuation of headline in the second line takes away the appeal.

Now that you have an idea of what a customer wants, you can get the dream machines going with an effective ad.

Ready Ad Gallery and Ready Image Ads

In 2013, an incredible new feature was made part of Google Adwords, which were the ready Ad Gallery and the Ready Image Ads feature.

To optimize your search engine efforts you must display such advertisements which are captivating in context and display such content that automatically captures the attention of your target audience. Creating innovative, compelling, and stunning requires a time, effort, and attention. The Ready Creatives feature made part of Google Adwords allows advertisers to make impressive and creative advertisements, which are displayed on a consistent basis across all screens. The feature is quite easy to use and enables you to make the advertisements as you want.

All you have to do is click on the option of "create new ad" and Google will immediately scan your page, as well as your website, and offer you various suggestions by creating a portfolio of HTML5 and Flash advertisements, in various dimensions, giving you a freer hand in deciding which advertisement to go with.

You can add images as you want, and even edit text to display your core message to the consumer or target audience. You can make use of the editor to create customized advertisements and make changes as you deem fit. Or you can select an already created template and use that.

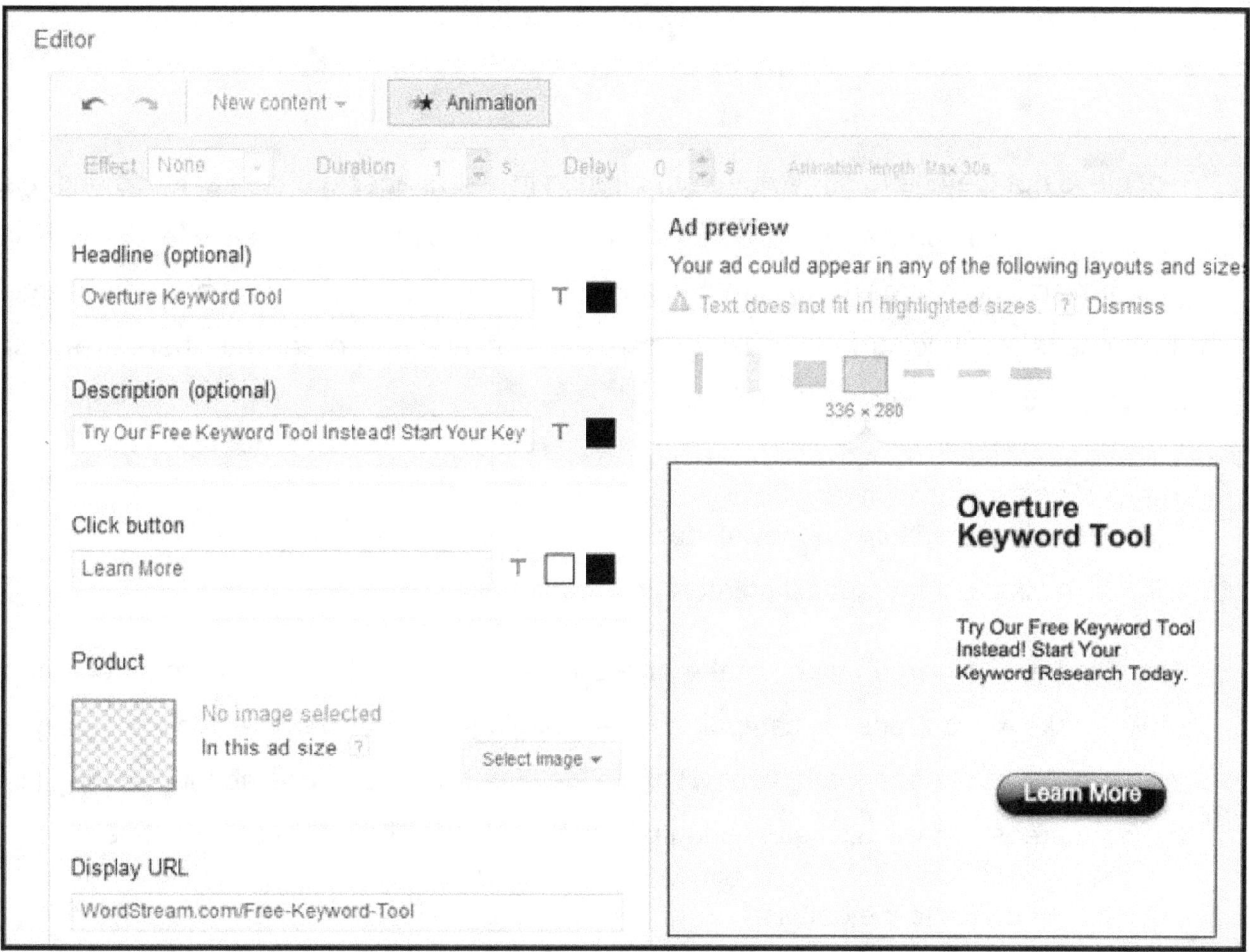

Chapter 06: Numbers That Matter - Google's Conversion Tracking Tells What Works and What Does Not

Google is not the one to shy away from offering its users absolute convenience and that is where conversion tracking steps in. This free tool can elevate the effectiveness of your advertising campaign to new heights as you will be able to find how your target audience is responding to your ads. Once a customer clicks on an ad, there are three things that can happen:

i.   He purchases the product
ii.   He signed up for your newsletter
iii. He filled a form requesting more information

The numbers delivered by any of the above-listed actions will help you get a good idea of which keywords, ads or campaigns are bringing you business and contributing to your growth. In the aftermath, you will make well-informed decisions about investing into the right areas and will ultimately end up boosting your ROI (Return on Investment).

Let's take a dive into the details.

What Is Conversion?

A conversion is simply an action a prospect performs on your website that offers your business some sort of value. It is called so because a click made by a customer on your website translates (or converts) to business.

Why Use Conversion Tracking?

Because sale is not the single metric you should be concerned with. In order to keep on improving your advertising campaigns, the following has to be achieved.

a) Alignment of keywords and ads with business goals

b) Improvement in ROI

These can be effortlessly achieved with the conversion tracking tool that Google AdWords has to offer. Simply put, if you are not using conversion tracking, you have no idea what you are missing.

How Google AdWords Conversion Tracking Help You Grow?

1) It helps you to find out how much you are getting out of your investment.
2) It helps you to identify areas that justify spending.
3) It assists you in determining the most profitable adgroups, campaigns and keywords.
4) It provides the means to test conversion page and ads in a faster and more effective manner.
5) It helps businesses to find out how much each visitor costs.
6) It helps determine any leaks that exist in one's website or landing page.

Types of Conversions

Before one sets out to use the tool, it is important to understand the two metrics that can be used for conversion tracking.

Conversion (1-Per-Click)

In this case, the tool will count a conversion for each ad click that lead to a conversion within a period of 30 days. This means that if, following a single click, more than one conversion happens, they will not be counted. They are ideal for counting acquisitions from unique customers such as sign-ups or leads.

Conversions (Many-Per-Click)

With this option, the tool counts each conversion made followed by an ad click. This implies that if more than one conversion occurs after a single click, they will all be counted individually. This is effective for assessing conversions that are valuable for a business every single time such as purchases.

How Conversion Tracking Works

What actually happens is that a snippet of JavaScript code or HTML is added to the webpage while ensuring that performance does not suffer. This snippet is usually placed such that they are displayed after a conversion has completed for instance, the 'Thank You' page.

When a customer clicks on an ad on Google.com or any other Google network websites, a cookie is stored on the prospect's computer temporarily. It is this cookie that records a conversion when a prospect lands on the conversion page.

Setting up Conversion Tracking

To set up conversion tracking, the following are needed.

   i.   A Google AdWords account

  ii.   A website

 iii.   The ability to edit the website

The two steps that follow are as follows.

   a) Get the code snippet

   b) Placement of code in the website's HTML

More Advanced Conversion Reporting

At the end of February, new terms were added in Google Adwords, which were immediately visible to the users, the moment they logged into the Adwords account. Previously there used to be columns of conversions (one per click) and conversions (many per click), which used to tell the rate at which the visitors to a user's website converted and the number of visitors who had successfully been converted. Now these columns have been replaced by, the columns of converted clicks and conversions.

This is a completely new way of finding out the conversion rates of visitors or potential customers. This advanced feature helps the users in providing businesses the flexibility they need to report on the things, which are important for their business.

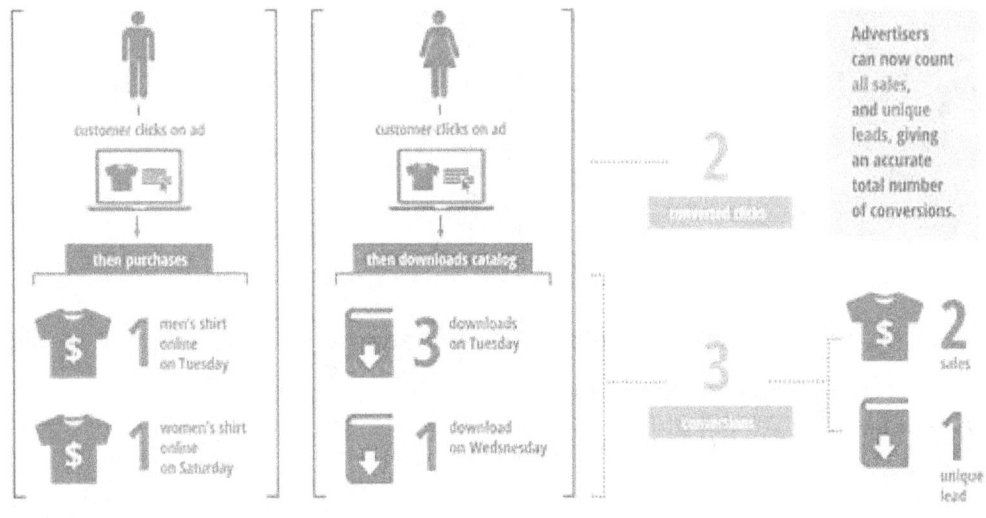

TAKE CONTROL OF HOW YOU COUNT CONVERSIONS

Berkeley T-shirts wants to count two different kinds of conversions in AdWords: sales and leads. They would like to count **every sale** driven by AdWords and **unique leads** like a download of one of their many catalogs.

Update in Conversion Values

The conversion values get updated without actually having any effect on the conversion tag. It is important to understand that not all of the conversions have the same value. Users have the ability to assign different values to different conversions, thereby, allowing them to be seen along different conversions, in their total value.

This advanced features helps the advertisers gain better understanding of what their customers are looking for, thereby, gaining access to better insights. It is also an effective method of gaining results through better reporting standards. Previously Google Adwords only used to record the number of conversions, which took place, while now they can see better reporting of their conversion rates.

Changing conversion values has become extremely easy and simple now. Follow the steps provided below, to change the conversion values.

1. Click on the tools tab given on the dashboard, and then select conversions from it.
2. Click on and sleet an existing conversion, in which you want to add some value.
3. For an action, which already exists, click on the tab labeled "Settings", then click on the option, which says "Edit Settings". This will allow you to enter a numeric value, which will be allotted to the conversion.
4. Choose the option of "Each Conversion has the same value," enter a number, and Save, by clicking on its button.

There is no need to update the tag, any value, which is assigned to the tag, will be ignored and the value you have selected and input previously, will replace the value in the tag.

Competitive Metrics Specific to Devices

Users have always had the option of seeing how well their ads are performing, by understanding the different metrics, and seeing where their advertisements stands with regards to competitors. However, this was only possible to view on desktop PCs. Now, Google has updated this feature to include auction insight reports which are device specific, users can determine where they are falling short against competitors, and the areas which require more effort and attention. this helps the users to take decisions which are data driven, based on one or the other consumer insight, thereby, helping make changes which have a positive impact on the user's business.

Organic versus Paid Reports

This change helps you in optimizing and analyzing the search footprint of your website on Google. Before the introduction of this update your paid and organic performance was shown separately. With this change, you will be able to gauge the consumer insights in a much efficient and effective manner. This report allows you to compare your performance with regard to a query. It also shows you the overlap between the paid and organic search responses, thereby giving you a better understanding of the consumer. It shows you the results of an ad, or organic listing, or both, when appear because of a search on Google. All those who have an Adwords account can benefit greatly from this. The biggest benefit gained through this report is that the businesses have a chance at discovering additional keywords, which the consumer might have used to search for your products or services.

In addition, it allows you to optimize the high value queries and use it to improve the presence of your business/ products/ services, etc, while allowing you to monitor all of your search engine optimization efforts. It also allows you to monitor and understand the impact of various promotional efforts as well as budget or keyword changes.

Campaigns	Ad groups	Settings	Ads	Keywords	Audiences	Ad extensions	Dimensions	Display Network	▾

View: Paid & organic ▾ | Filter ▾ | Columns ▾ | ↓

Query	Ad stats					Organic stats					Combined ad and organic stats		
	Clicks	Impr.	CTR	Avg. CPC	Avg. Pos	Clicks	Queries	Clicks/query	Listings/query	Avg. Pos	Clicks	Queries	Clicks/query
google analytics training	29	421	6.89%	$14.01	1.4	13	412	3.15%	1.2	6.3	42	421	9.98%
Ad shown only	0	9	0.00%	$0.00	1.8	0	0	0.00%	0.0	0.0	0	9	0.00%
Both shown	29	412	7.04%	$14.01	1.4	13	412	3.15%	1.2	6.3	42	412	10.19%
google adwords training	11	144	7.64%	$10.33	1.2	2	34	5.88%	1.1	5.9	13	144	9.03%
Ad shown only	4	110	3.64%	$10.57	1.2	0	0	0.00%	0.0	0.0	4	110	3.64%
Both shown	7	34	20.59%	$10.19	1.1	2	34	5.88%	1.1	5.9	9	34	26.47%
lunametrics	9	119	7.56%	$0.92	1.0	72	118	61.02%	6.9	1.0	81	119	68.07%
Ad shown only	0	1	0.00%	$0.00	1.0	0	0	0.00%	0.0	0.0	0	1	0.00%
Both shown	9	118	7.63%	$0.92	1.0	72	118	61.02%	6.9	1.0	81	118	68.64%
adwords training	5	91	5.49%	$14.15	1.5	1	30	3.33%	1.7	6.0	6	91	6.59%
Ad shown only	4	61	6.56%	$14.25	1.5	0	0	0.00%	0.0	0.0	4	61	6.56%
Both shown	1	30	3.33%	$13.73	1.3	1	30	3.33%	1.7	6.0	2	30	6.67%

Consumer Ratings

These annotations highlight industry specific ratings. These consumer ratings are based on consumer surveys. The three best ratings, which you receive, are shown below the search ads text, which also consists of a link. Clicking on this link will take you to further ratings.

These consumer ratings, or annotations, help in driving the traffic to your website. This traffic is based on consumer opinion.

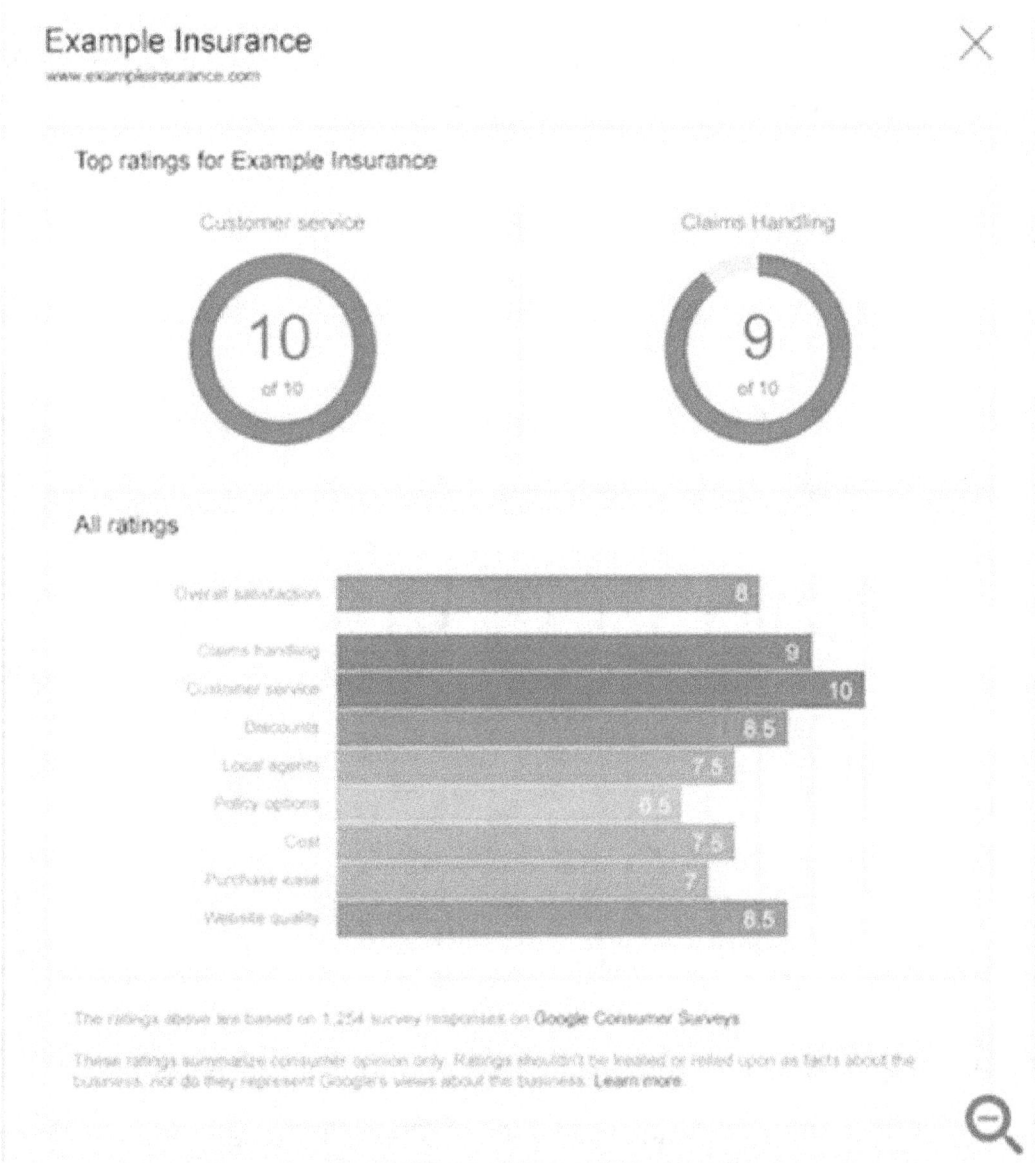

Bidding Options

With the introduction of the enhanced campaigns, it has become easier to bid in a more versatile nature. Now advertisers have the option of bidding higher or lower for clicks. These clicks are based on the time, device, and location of the searcher, thereby preventing the advertiser from creating different campaigns for different locations, and devices.

These enhanced campaigns have brought different types of changes, one of which allows the advertiser check the conversion ratio of potential consumers through mobile advertising. The option also allows you to add simulator columns for your bids, regarding your keywords report. This action immediately allows you to view and analyze multiple keywords estimates.

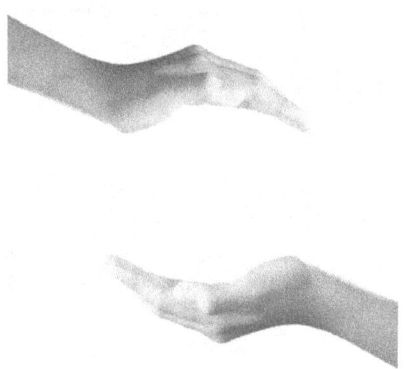

Base max. CPC ?	Est. add. clicks/wk (-50% bid) ?	Est. add. clicks/wk (+50% bid) ?	Est. add. clicks/wk (+300% bid) ?	Est. add. clicks/wk (top page bid) ?	Est. add. cost/wk (-50% bid) ?	Est. add. cost/wk (+50% bid) ?	Est. add. cost/wk (+300% bid) ?	Est. add. cost/wk (top page bid) ?
$0.60	-24	201	253	51	-$56.23	$588.78	$805.79	$138.61

Security and Privacy

Security standards enforced by Google are strict. Only those pages are tracked by these tools that have the conversion code embedded in them. Also, secure servers and data encryption are used to guarantee confidentiality. To top it all, the following guidelines are followed to safeguard customer data.

1) Servers for search results are separate from those used for conversion tracking.
2) Cookies used for conversion tracking persist for a specific time period only.
3) It is not possible to link conversion data to individual customers. Data displayed is for overall keywords and ads.
4) Options are provided to notify customers about cookies.

As we conclude this chapter, it is worth-mentioning that the ability to measure results can help any advertising campaign excel. This added tool offered by Google AdWords makes it a platform that has empowered businesses to secure the kind of success that go well beyond one's expectations.

The Final Word

Google AdWords may be a buzz for some businesses that is soon going to fade. However, what these businesses fail to understand is that Google AdWords is no longer just an effort to go an extra mile. It can have lasting impressions on your business' advertising strategy and can be the first step for a business to write its success story.

Leverage the power of Google AdWords as it not only drives results, it creates value for your business. By using the proficient and invaluable tool expertly, you will not only secure scores of new customers but will be able to strengthen your existing client-base as well.

Are You Ready To Transform Your Business From 'NO-THING' To The 'NEXT BIG THING'? Want To Secure That Proverbial 'Success Overnight'? Use Google Adwords And Watch The Traffic Tempting Tool Earn Your Business The Spotlight.